AGING MINDFULLY, SOULFULLY and PEACEFULLY in the NEW POST-PANDEMIC ERA

A MESSAGE OF HOPE

To Leila

Enjoy!

Don

By

Don Ayre

July 9/21

AGING MINDFULLY, SOULFULLY and PEACEFULLY in the NEW POST-PANDEMIC ERA

A MESSAGE OF HOPE

Copyright © 2021 by Don Ayre

ISBN: 978-0-9686561-7-4

All Rights Reserved

TABLE OF CONTENTS

ACKNOWLEGEMENTS

I'd like to thank my son Ramon for his editing assistance and as my technical consultant in the creation of this book. I also want to thank Nick Caya and his team at www.Word-2-kindle.com who made publishing my book in both ebook and print on demand formats on Amazon.com a reality.

INTRODUCTION: A SERIES OF 4D AWARENESS PAPERS

Due to the fact that COVID-19 has laid bare our vulnerability as a global community and indeed our continued survival as a species if we don't mend our ways at every level of existence - physicals, intellectual, emotional and spiritual, I am going to offer what I call 4D AWARENESS PAPERS. They are the best that I can do using my past training and experience as a researcher and practitioner in the field of child and family therapy and community development to sort the steady flow of information that is coming my way. They are more intended as sketches than works of art or in any sense of completion. And so they are at best are glimpses of our cosmic reality given the limitations of the place and time that defines my present perspective...but they open the way to dialogue.

The research requirement as we turn the corner to navigate the future is enormous but so is our ability to respond to the demand. But it will take the informed 4D AWARENESS of each one of us as members of the global community. It's up to us to be both SELF and WORLD aware and to assure ourselves that our growth and development both personally and politically is aligned with a cosmic reality. Hence, the term "4D awareness papers."

Thus 4D AWARENESS PAPERS gathered here as chapters for this book were originally position papers developed as an extension of some of my earlier writings BEYOND MINDFULNESS AND SOULFULNESS. I posted them on my website over the past few months but having rewritten and revised them several times, I have found that they have evolved to the point that a reader should be able to see the COVID-19 in a different and more positive light aimed at personal and political recovery. A book emerged. Without such writings, I believe that we won't be able to unravel the present situation being left in the wake of COVID-19 and gather ourselves together to make the transition to a post COVID-19 era.

It is most important post COVID-19 to get BEYOND MINDFULNESS AND SOULFULNESS to PEACEFULNESS as a new platform for building a global community that is consistent with cosmic reality. Otherwise, we will miss what's just around the corner of our future. In hindsight, we could have seen COVID-19 coming had we been open to its possibility.

But all that aside, we can move on by developing a very different sense of our SELVES and the WORLD around us simply by recognizing that two streams of learning MINDFULNESS and SOULFULNESS and combining them. We have already been learning this about ourselves as individuals from a MINDFULNESS perspective and to some extent from a SOULFULNESS perspective but we are slow to start the 4D learning as societies. COVID-19 has caught us unawares. We need a new 4D way of looking at life and of understanding ourselves and the world around us, if for no other reason than to see beyond what the news media and other political influences bring forward via television and the internet. This new awareness seems to be happening with the assistances of new technologies, but none too soon.

We need a new, more comprehensive way of looking at life. There are four most basic questions that we ask ourselves as we go through life, even as from birth - *Who am I? What's the world around me all about? Where do I fit in?* and *Why are we here?* If we are not constantly aware of these four dimensions of living and open, balanced, integrated and progressive in our outlook, we find ourselves participating in and contributing to a world for ourselves that is not what we want, one that is at best lopsided and out-of-sync with nature itself. And then we wonder...

It could be argued that all of this is self-fulfilling process. But that's exactly the point. I'd much sooner be guided by the inner sense of my humanity than that of someone else. Even more by an inner sense of humanity that is balanced and integrated and open to dialogue. For this reason, I have prepared this book and will continue to present my four dimensional thinking as I adjust to my aging in the new POST-PANDEMIC ERA. My ongoing efforts at 4D AWARENESS PAPERS can be found on my website entitled BEYOND MINDFULNESS AND SOULFULNESS at donayre.ca

CHAPTER 1 - MEDITATION, MANTRAS AND OPEN-MINDEDNESS

For me, meditation was more than a 1970s fad. It was an open window into our awareness of the cosmic realities of our existence and within that a basis of meeting of minds, Western with Eastern thought and globally. In fact, it had opened my mind in ways I could never have imagined had I stayed within the confines of my growing up as a middle class Canadian and of my becoming disciplined professionally as a Family and Child Therapist.

I had pretty much followed along with what was required but all the while, being always conscious of somehow being of two minds, the one tapped into the learning stream of all that was important to me in maintaining a level of success in the world around me and the other tapped into the learning stream of all that was important to me in being "me" and happy at it. There was even a little conversation going on in me all the time to balance the two streams of learning. In fact, it's that way with all of us. It depends on how aware we are of it.

To free myself up to study meditation and have an expanded awareness of this ongoing process in my life, I eventually went into private practice as family and child therapist and community development consultant. Over the twenty five years that I was a consultant, my use of meditation evolved. More and more, I began to recognize that meditation was a process, that I was going and taking my clients through a four stage process that was responsive to four basic life questions: 1) Who am I? 2) What's Life All About? 3) Where do I fit in? and 4) Why are we here? I wrote this up in two self-published books: 1) Meditation and the Emergence of Cosmic Consciousness; and Towards a More Loving and Caring World.

Then seven years ago, my use of meditation became even more personal and more convincing. I discovered that I could use meditation as a means of developing a personalized mantra! My wife, Jean, and I had moved from our home of 46 years in a suburb of Winnipeg, Manitoba, Canada to a retirement community. It was a major adjustment but we were both in our 80s and ready for the move. We were fortunate. It happened quickly and easily…the finding of a new location, the downsizing and moving from a house to an apartment in a retirement community, even the becoming a part of the new community. We had crossed a line and entered into a new lifestyle designed for the elderly. But ask anyone living in my community. We are adamant about it. Being elderly does not mean that we are "getting older." New lifestyle or not, "old" is not a word in our vocabulary. Rather, we are "ageing." I think what it means is that we accept age as a process not as a designation. But we don't like to go much further with it than that.

Almost immediately, Jean was elected president of the resident advisory board and continued to work at what she called "love's connectivity." Best as I can describe it thinking back to then is: "making the world a better place through more positive one-to-one relationships." She truly lived it and was quickly recognized for it. Whereas, I was slower to adjust. At her urging, I resumed my writing based on what I have called "human continuity." Sometimes, I've called it "love's generativity." Too clumsy a word for such a miraculous process. Regardless, I mean: "trying to understand the present world in the context of our common human destiny one generation to the next."

I had built my private practice as a family and child therapist and educational consultant around the concept of "love's continuity", whereas Jean's commitment to "love's connectivity" had made her well-respected for her career work as a counselor at the Manitoba Youth Centre. At home, Jean and I had learned to balance one another in our decision making. We were both very convinced that living was about loving and about learning in that context.

Now retired, we both felt that we were living in a world that was becoming too topsy-turvy. The global sense of community and beyond that, the universal sense of humanity that we had anticipated back when we were working just wasn't happening. We decided that we needed a day-by-day reminder that was more positive than what was being reported to us in the newspapers and through TV. More like what we had often times experienced. Eventually, we wrote what we considered to be a simple poem about our ongoing participation in and contribution toward a common human destiny that is more loving and caring.

> **Look for Beauty in all things,**
> **Expect Love at all time,**
> **Give from the Heart,**
> **Be grateful for Life itself,**
> **And SMILE...**

Looking back, the words seem idealistic but they were intended to challenge us to be continuously reaching out beyond where we were. We didn't know it at the time but we'd written a personal mantra based on our mutual experience. It was a lot of work but as it turned out, the poem proved to be especially important to us not only to maintain our optimism about life but also to express our gratitude for life itself. Just for the sake of clarity, I looked up Personal Mantra on Google:

"A Personal Mantra is an affirmation to motivate and inspire you to be your best self. It is typically a positive phrase or statement that you use to affirm the way you want to live your life. The true value of a mantra comes when it is audible, visible, and/or in your thoughts."

So what Jean and I and so many other people do by writing and rewriting their personal mantras is simply to make a progressive commitment to life that is visible to themselves and others as a basis for ongoing dialogue. It not only opens up the possibility of self-management through a renewed sense of self-consciousness, but also of mutual management through an extended awareness of the world around us. Nothing new, really. Seemingly not that difficult. Personal mantras simply mean an awareness of our own growth and development.

MINDFULNESS AND SOULFULNESS LEARNING. In addition to personal mantras, we had discovered within ourselves two distinct streams of learning: MINDFULNESS that is of particular interest to the left hemisphere of the brain and SOULFULNESS that is of particular interest to the right hemisphere of the brain. As a result, we can be four dimensional - material and intellectual from the left and emotional and spiritual from the right. But the hard part Jean and I knew from our relationship with one another and others is balancing these four dimensions of learning. We tend to emphasize one dimension or another. Most often, we tend to be four dimensional creatures living in a three dimensional world of our own making.

Mantras, then, are a means of our finding our way to the center of ourselves and to our at-oneness with our humanity. In terms of what is now known as Left-Brain and Right-Brain Theory, Jean was predominantly "a right-brained thinker." She was truly a master at what we both knew to be "connectivity." SOULFULNESS is the full extent of the right hemisphere of the brain. In contrast, I am predominantly "a left-brain thinker." MINDFULNESS is the full extent of the left brain. Remember though, we all have right and left hemispheres to our brains and that balancing the two is a constant and universal activity based on how well we are equipped to deal with life as we understand it at any given time and space.

So it turns out that it's not uncommon for people to write mantras - for balance. Specifically to balance left brain with right brain. To center themselves. Through the ages, there have been a lot mantras written. They are "out there" - in books, in songs, on the internet - for us to choose from and to pass on from one generation to the next - or we can build on their learning and write one of our own. It's up to us as individuals. I still use the one that Jean and I wrote but I am always finding others and trying to improve my mantra. Regardless of their practicality, mantras are universal and everlasting. In some mysterious way, they connect us eternally.

I don't know what prompted us to attempt a mantra at the particular time in our lives that we did. We had tried it before - somewhat successfully, we had felt. But this time there was an urgency - brought on perhaps by the combined pressures of our retiring and then moving to a new life-location. Also even though it was pre-COVID-19 times, there was enough going on in our lives and around us at the time that we were seeing some major disconnects that were bothering us. For Jean it was more social justice issues that bothered her. For me, it was more ecological ones. We'd both been very active with our respective concerns and supportive of one another but now that we were retired, we felt more like spectators.

Or maybe it was that we were anticipating things to come? Sometimes that happens. There is enough evidence to believe that universal premonitions do happen and we can pick up on warnings written into our common sense of humanity. Maybe an awareness of this was intensifying for Jean and me as we entered the ageing process? Regardless, we felt the need for a stronger mantra.

We were able to complete it in time for the book launching of my book Toward a More Loving and Caring World. No, I don't know if it works for anyone else. Some say "yes"; some say "no". But regardless, it worked for Jean and me. And it still works for me.

AGEING. Five years after we moved into the retirement community, life's ailments caught up with us and our mantra was even more comforting to us. We had moved into the retirement community, not because we were retired so much as we needed the support of independent living. I had had cancer and was recovering. Jean was on the waiting-list for a hip replacement but it was doubtful that she would get it due to a heart defect from birth. Five years after we moved in, Jean was in the hospital critically ill but eventually released into palliative care with the option of medical assistance in dying.

On December 23, 2018, Jean chose to die with dignity in our apartment with family and friends. Because of her exemplary braveness in the face of death and loving words for us all, my family encouraged me to write a book about Jean. I did. I called it: "The Power of Love's Connectivity: A Case Study in Medical Assistance in Dying." But truly it was a love story. Our mantra was a great help to the two of us, especially when she was in palliative care. It continues to be a great help after she chose to die with dignity.

It seems that mantras are not only a means of getting to the core of our lives and centering ourselves but they open up a window into an ever-expanding view of life and discovery. It takes beyond what we know - beyond MINDFULNESS and SOULFULNESS to PEACEFULNESS, if we are willing. I even have the mantra that Jean and I wrote almost five years ago posted on the door of my apartment and on my walker not only as a reminder to myself but also as a sort of conversation piece. It's especially important to me now that I am midway into the pandemic being caused by the COVID-19 virus.

Needless to say, the need to remind and reassure myself by listening to the small voice inside myself is higher than ever before. None of us even have the benefits of family and friends visiting! So COVID-19 is already changing our lives in ways previously unimaginable. And even when it is contained, it will continue to change our lives. Life will never be the same for any of us. We will need a new acceptance and understanding of what's BEYOND MINDFULNESS AND SOULFULNESS.

So it's not just by happen chance that it's become one of the tools that I use to balance what I call my MINDFULNESS and SOULFULNESS learning on a daily basis. It brings me an almost immediate sense of PEACEFULNESS. MINDFULNESS is what goes on in the LEFT hemisphere of the brain whereas SOULFULNESS is what goes on in the RIGHT side of the brain. Somehow these two powerful streams of learning are brought together as one. But how? How can we better manage this inner force of our humanity? Mantras will get us "there" but what do we do when we arrive?

CHAPTER 2 - MINDFULNESS, SOULFULNESS AND THE AMAZING BALANCING AND INTEGRATING POWER OF THE CORPUS CALLOSUM

Because of my years as a researcher in support of my private practice as a family and child therapist and community development consultant, I'm comfortable with words like MINDFULNESS and SOULFULNESS to translate the recent findings of neurobiologists and other related professionals. Clearly, it all gets back to the fact that the brain is a living organism with a LEFT and RIGHT hemispheres that are in constant interaction. Hence, two streams of learning.

But I don't think that the name that they have given to the organ that integrates our learning and the growth and development that is ongoing does justice to it. They call it a CORPUS CALLOSUM. But because of my research background and experience in practice as family and child therapist and community development consultant, I prefer to call it the LOVE LINK. It's what enables us to work together.

When I was in private practices as a therapist, I used to suggest the use of a different mantra, one that was more generic. I suggested the daily asking of life's four basic questions:

Who am I?

What's life all about?

Where do I fit in?

Why are we here?

Somehow, those four questions have been found to stimulate the mind and to open it to the changes that come with the mutual dialogue basic to therapy. Just by running our minds through these questions, we make ourselves increasingly more conscious of ourselves. A mantra simply formalizes this internal questioning.

Mostly we don't take the time out to think through these four most basis questions - not the answers but the questions themselves - routinely and at some depth to set in motion all life's learning at our disposal. We don't have a balanced perspective to include the physical, intellectual, emotional and even spiritual. It turns out that the first two lines of this generic mantra speak to the physical and intellectual dimensions of our living and that the second two speak to the emotional and spiritual dimensions of our living. They are like "hot buttons" stimulating our understanding of all four dimensions at once and facilitating the magical work of what neuroscientists call the CORPUS CALLOSUM. Again, my preference would be to call it the LOVE LINK.

In fact, the thinking behind mantras is pretty straight forward. It seems that at the start of life, we are gifted with a body and a brain that has two hemispheres - a LEFT and a RIGHT. These two hemisphere combine to create a four dimensional view of life - physical, mental, emotional and spiritual. The LEFT hemisphere is more cognizant of what goes on physically and mentally; the RIGHT hemisphere is more interested in what happens to us emotionally and spiritually. What we make of life depends on the mix. As a result, the instant by instant work of the CORPOS CALLOSUM or LOVE LINK has an enormous influence on our lives 1) it arranges a working partnership between the LEFT and RIGHT hemispheres of our brains 2) it connects the expression of this MINDFULNESS and

SOULFULNESS effectively with the world around us and 3) it continuously expands our awareness and contributes to our ongoing growth and development.

KEEPING ONE'S SELF BALANCED. Personal mantras are best designed to "speak" the languages of both hemisphere and to facilitate the mixing process of the CORPOS CALLOSUM or LOVE LINK in that way we are kept in balance as "productive" versus "creative" individuals. We are as a result, "successful" versus "happy" as contributing members. More so, if the particular society we participate in is align with humanity as a whole.

Regardless, mantras promote the magic of mixing the four dimensions of life as we experience them and shape our perspective. How we do this very personally and very experimentally depends on our life circumstances and on our optimism about life. It's difficult to participate in and contribute to a more loving and caring world, if it's not what we are experiencing. And it's not what we are experiencing, if it's not what we are looking for. It's to us to make it happen. Thus personal mantras are more than just reminders, they are what brings us together as societies and ultimately a humanity. Increasingly, MINDFULNESS and SOULFULNESS become one and eventually we can go about our lives PEACEFULLY. Sounds too simple. True enough. We've got a lot of learning to do.

There other ways of bringing the integrated powers of both streams of learning - mind and soul - together as one, of course. Art, music, intuitions about life, what we recognize as the inner insights about life. But it seems that for the first three or four years, our learning about life is more open-minded and goes on mainly in the right hemisphere. Then the more cautionary learning of the left hemisphere steps into driver's seat. Instead of balancing the four dimensions of our learning about life - physical, mental, emotional and spiritual, we find it easier to make sense out what we are combined learning of all four dimensions by relegating the spiritual dimension to the back seat. This continues for the rest of our lives and meets with success, except that we are not totally happy. So it important that we are constantly aware of the inner dialogue that goes on between our MINDFULNESS learning and our SOULFULNESS learning as life goes on. More, it is important that we keep ourselves balanced. Open to MINDFULNESS, yes. Open to SOULFULNESS, yes. Open to what's beyond the two combined, also yes.

Recent research in all fields suggests that this is exactly what are brains are designed for! Our lives are a continuous balancing act, being challenged and thrown off course and then recovering, changing and growing in the process. It's the interaction of MINDFULNESS and SOULFULNESS resolving as one - PEACEFULNESS - which we are continuously striving toward nanosecond by nanosecond. The point is to be as aware as possible of the process and living it. It is best known to us as "Going with the flow." it is best known as.

In short, researchers using today's technology to map its structure and functioning, now recognize that our brains include in their structure and functioning an innate healing quality that researchers call "altruistic love" Increasingly, the evidence tells them that "altruistic love" is an innate quality that seeks expression in our growth as individuals - but it has be nurtured through experience. Thus societies need to provide opportunities to be "compassionate" not only to allow individuals to participate in and contribute to a world that is healthy but also to continue to be healthy itself. It's almost like having exercises for the brain as well as for the body.

AGEING and SELF-REVIEW. As so many of us enter into what researchers are calling the "ageing process," the need to balance the physical, intellectual, emotional and spiritual dimensions of our lives intensifies and becomes at matter of individual choice. Thus meditation that links altruistic love interactively with compassion is highly recommended by researchers as it promotes the growth and development of new cells. The left sides of our brains become less dominant and the right hemispheres are more insistent. A more four dimensional outlook develops to accommodate this by the introduction of what is perceived as a stronger "sense of spirituality." In very, very short order, we begin to convert our knowledge into wisdom.

The recent research even goes so far as to suggest that this might be the purpose and meaning of "ageing," both for us as individuals and family members and also for society as a whole. It would seem to explain the common experiences of most people as they grow older and begin to experience "ageing." Ironically the situation created for us personally and dealt with by our societies globally works against this. Instead of being freed from the time/space demands of our living, we are preoccupied. Medical issues predominate. Naturally, we are concerned personally and society responds politically by placing us in environments that maximize physical care while making sure that we are otherwise entertained and content. It is very difficult for us to balance the four dimensions of our lives without considerable effort of awareness.

I recall that when Jean and I wrote the personal mantra that I shared earlier in this paper, we were just moving into Portsmouth Retirement Community. So clearly, it reflected not only our previous experience with mantras based on life's most basic questions: Who? What?

Where? and Why? but also the urgency of present place in time/space. It was a matter of our mutual growth and development. We therefore found the writing of it very challenging to say the very least. Partly it was the word but most it was because it demanded constant change of us. However, it brought us many moments of PEACEFULNESS as we were able to pause long enough and often enough to step out of the bus-i-ness of our daily lives. Without knowing it, we covered off all four dimensions of our lives and spoke the language of both side of our brains.

1. **The Physical Dimensions - Look for beauty in all things**

2. **The Intellectual Dimension - Expect love at all times**

3. **The Emotional Dimension - Share from the heart**

4. **The Spiritual Dimension - Be grateful for life itself**

5. **The Integration of all four dimension - And SMILE.**

Through mantras and other means of creativity, we position ourselves in the midst of our productive and creative lives and enjoy the energy flow of its four dimensions as one. There are many ways of tapping into both sides of our brains. But first and foremost, we are going to have to take the time and find the places to let the positive side of our humanity find its full expression. Considering the massive confusion that COVID-19 virus is causing us, sorting out our MINDFULNESS learning from our SOULFULNESS learning and then integrating them as PEACEFULNESS is not going to be easy.

In fact, we all are going to have to move BEYOND MINDFULNESS and SOULFULNESS. One or the other won't work. So we are left with the question: How? It will take some very new and different ways of looking at life, ourselves, our families, our communities, and even beyond that, at the entire world around us including our life here on planet earth and our place in the universe.

There never will be a single answer to that single question: How? But obviously it's going to be up to us as individuals. So the new discovery that we are going to have to be more aware of is ourselves as four dimensional - body, mind, heart and spirit. In particular, it's the new discovery of a brain with left and right hemispheres that constantly struggle within each one of us to see the world around us as an integrated whole and to build a four dimensional version of it - physical, emotional, intellectual and spiritual - that is universally aligned. Fortunately, there is another new discovery that is enabling the brain. Coincidentally, it's the discovery of the Internet.

We are in this time/space on the planet together. We have connectivity with one another and with nature itself. And we have continuity from one generation to the next and within the universe. It is vitally important that we keep our learning from both sources balanced and open to the growth and development of our inner humanity and to its outward expression in even the smallest acts of kindness and compassion. Regardless, mantras are the meeting places of our humanity, collectively and one generation to the next. They bring to life a four dimensional vision of ourselves and life around us - physical, intellectual, emotional and spiritual - that is tomorrow's world.

In short, mantras reposition us at the center of our lives and help us to renew our sense of self-leadership. It is, after all, our life that we are living out and the more we remind ourselves of this in the wash of information and ongoing problems that come at us in the course of a day, the better. Otherwise, we are prone to be misled by others personally, politically and even commercially. The lifestyle that we develop is not what we want. Hence, protests. But really, transformation and change can only come from within ourselves as we band together to work towards an ever-greater sense of humanity. In this sense, mantras can become a powerful four dimensional when we are working together to remind us of our commitment to more loving and caring world.

CHAPTER 3 - BALANCING LEFT BRAIN VERSUS RIGHT BRAIN LEARNING

So much of what we learn is experiential and is spent in recovering from LEFT BRAIN versus RIGHT BRAIN imbalance that we feel almost constantly off-guard. After I lost Jean, I went through a long period of recovery. Once my assorted doctors had figured out which pains to treat first, it came down to sciatica and eventually spinal synopsis. I had apparently managed somehow to minimize the effects of these medical problems while we got ourselves through the palliative care period of our lives and enjoy the moments that we had together.

The medical problems that I had that surfaced afterward were too far advanced, except drugs. But while the drugs relieved the pain but they cost me a fair amount of my cognitive functions. This is a familiar pattern in most people in their later years and are defined as elderly. However, I was fortunate to have a medical delivery person who worked with me. He was trained as a nurse practitioner and capable of doing everything a trained doctors does with the exception of surgeries. He also had a different approach to the delivery of medications…more related to my ongoing comfort care than to than to an immediate cure and more holistic. He operated out of his car and made home visits. But relied on referrals to specialists. He was qualified to use all of the usual testing that was preliminary to referrals. When he layered in my drugs for spinal synopsis, he stayed in touch with me and my pharmacist by phone and could make immediate adjustments until must the right amount for my ailment and my body were being administered.

On his advice, I tried to recover my cognitive powers by making myself do certain things - like drawing and writing. In particular,

I tried to draw a self-portrait by using a pencil to sketch the picture of my on the back of my book, Toward a More Loving and Caring World. The results were dismal. Even with many erasures and adjustments, I couldn't get my self-portrait to look the way I wanted to. I'd never been very good at pencil sketching in the first place so I was about to give up when I noticed something strange. The eye glasses that I was drawing onto my self-portrait were not the ones on the picture on the back of my book. They were the ones that I was wearing today. I went and double checked in the mirror. Sure enough. Right eye glasses for today but wrong eye glasses for a picture on the back of a book that was 10 years old! I redrew my self-portrait. It was remarkable improved. Strange?!

A few afternoons later, I was attending an art class provided as one of the recreational programs at my retirement community. I mentioned my experience to a fellow art student. She left the classroom to get something that she wanted to show me. She returned very excited with a book called Drawing on the Right side of the Brain. The author, Betty Edwards, described how we don't draw what we see. We draw what we THINK we see. I was looking at my picture on the back of my book but drawing the updated version! Betty Edwards has developed a school in California based on this. The right brain hemisphere sees but the left hemisphere of the brain thinks it sees. The trick in art is to free the right brain up to express itself. Similarly with writing. Writing is also a form of art. We sketch ideas in our heads even on paper via "doodling.' In either case, we don't draw what we see; we draw what we think we see.

As my excited fellow student went on to explain all of this to me, my memory flipped back to an experience I had had in grade school. It had discouraged me for life from art. I was criticized in grade v for having attempted to draw a book that I had read recently. I attempted to draw Moby Dick. But I was told that there was no such thing as a white whale. End of. I made several fun attempts at art as an adult but I was never too successful and always sensitive to criticism. However, my attending the art class offered by the retirement community had been fairly successful. And my art had improved immeasurably. The book my fellow student had brought to me took me into another world of achievement altogether! I recovered no only my ability to draw but also and most important to me as a former researcher, my abilities to read and write.

I have yet to complete the course of studies outlined in this amazing book, Drawing on the Right Side of the Brain. However, I am already benefiting from it and other studies. It turns out that in common to us all is the vast difference between and amazing coordination of the Left hemisphere versus the Right hemisphere of our brains such that we learning from both sides of our brains. In fact, the two hemispheres of our brains differ so significantly that there is a constant dialogue going on within us as we struggle continuously to maintain a balanced outlook on life. Hence, we are always "talking" to ourselves, the inner voice within us with the outer voice of others. We are always seeking a balanced outlook of the four basic dimensions of our selves - physical, intellectual, emotional and spiritual.

The Left hemisphere of the brain is more verbal, analytical, and orderly than the Right hemisphere, so much so that researchers in the field of neuro-biology more often called it "the digital brain." It's better at things like reading, writing, and computations. Most importantly, it loves to categorize our learning. As a result, it is connected to logic, sequencing, linear thinking, mathematics, facts and thinking in words. In short, it pays attention to what's happening in the physical and intellectual dimensions of our lives. It makes us successful.

The Right Hemisphere of the brain is more visual and intuitive. Again, neuro-biologists have given it a name – "the analogue brain." It has a more creative and less organized way of thinking. It is also connected to imagination, holistic thinking, intuition, arts, rhythm, nonverbal cues, feelings, visualization and daydreaming. In short, it pays more attention to what's going on in the emotional and spiritual dimensions of our lives. Its activity relates to our happiness.

In this way, the Left side of the brain is more interested in what's going on in our lives materially and intellectually; the right is more likely to pay attention to what's happening emotionally and spiritually. So on the one side, we're being flooded by sensations and thoughts; on the other, we're dealing with feelings and intuitions. And all of this takes place repeatedly in nanoseconds to process our experiences and store them in memory banks of our brains! Faster than we are even aware of it going on. In short, our brains like our bodies and for the most part in concert with them are in a constant state of growth and development. Today's neuro-scientists call it the brain's "plasticity."

LEFT BRAIN VERSUS RIGHT BRAIN DEVELOPMENT. For the first three years or life, learning follows the pattern of the child in the uterus. For as yet unknown reasons, it is able to us transfer of feelings and intuitions and flows interactively child to mother giving priority to bottom up. It is mainly what we call the right brain's activity, remembered and retained as such. At three or so, the child's learning has finished its translation of this early learning into the ways of the world and learning is shifted to left brain. Its learning tends to flow from the top down.

Once the left brain takes over, it pretty much carries us to retirement. It's called education or more recently, "lifelong learning." Then the right brain has to be caught up. As a result of this two brained development process, we are four dimensional creatures (physical, intellectual, emotional and spiritual) living in a three dimensional world of our own making but not necessary in synch with our origins.

The SELF is eager to take in information about the new world it finds itself in; society that represents the new world is keen to teach and help the self in the new learning process. This is the function of the left hemisphere. The right hemisphere is open ended. Meanwhile, the two hemispheres of our brains are significantly different to the point that we require some sort of combination of the two that is, if we are make decisions and function in ways that keep up with it all and lead toward both success and happiness. How is this possible?

The key to making the left and right brains working together is what today's neuro-biologists refer to as the CORPOS CALLOSUM. It's a large belt of millions and millions of cells joining the two hemispheres of our brains. Its primary function is to integrate motor, sensory, and cognitive performances between the cerebral cortex on one side of the brain to the same region on the other side. As a result of its activity, the two hemispheres are coordinated and hopefully harmonized. This means that, since each hemisphere informs us of two dimensions our ongoing interactions with the world around us, we are potentially four dimensional in our vision of life – physical and intellectual from the left side of our brains and emotional and spiritual dimensions from the right. Whereas given the developmental process that was described earlier in this article, we tend to see the world as three dimensional.

The discovery of the CORPOS CALLOSUM is recent. Maybe 100 years or so ago by neuro-biologists, especially by surgeons and other professionals dealing with injuries of the brain. Needless to say, researchers have been trying to find out more about this amazing part of the brain – about how it works and how we can make it function better. So up to now, research has been for the purposes of facilitating the medical interventions needed when the brain is damaged or unhealthy. But as technology has been advancing and made available to them, doctors and psychiatrists are beginning to apply this ongoing learning to the structure and functioning of the healthy brain as well. Regardless of the terminology, they are exploring the inner depths of the brain's structure and functional connectivity in ways that are useful to other professionals.

The good news is that there is a transmigration of information that is happening across the professions, nationally and internationally. It is leaving a trail of new knowledge and wisdom accessible to the general public not only on the self-help shelves of books stores and libraries but also on the internet! And so it is the learning of the left half of our brains versus the learning of the right half of our brains being brought together as one by the unique integrative powers of a CORPOS CALLOSUM that is so vitally important to how we restructure our living for tomorrow's world.

The CORPUS CALLOSUM is truly amazing. An example of the unique powers of the CORPUS CALLOSUM would be how we learn and perform music. Music is a highly technical skill that has to be learned and repeated over and over at different levels of understanding, even with different instruments and applications. First and foremost, it is a LEFT BRAIN activity. Thus music initially is very physical and intellectual and yet very personal as it reaches out intuitively to the emotions of others. And so it is very personal, even when we are on the receiving end of it. But when we perform, it is reaches out emotionally and even spiritually in the sense that it is appeals to the RIGHT BRAIN. When all four dimensions of learning are connected as one and executed, often the result is "inspirational."

Conversely when we listen to someone perform musically, we are critical via the LEFT BRAIN and the RIGHT BRAIN combined at all four dimensions of learning – physical, intellectual, emotional and spiritual. Thus music attracts us, connects with us, intrigues us with its complexity, inspires us…or it doesn't. It depends on both the LEFT BRAIN versus RIGHT BRAIN of the performer…and of the listener. Anyone who has experienced this kind of musical interchange has to marvel at the brain's functioning and, in particular, that of the CORPUS CALLOSUM. This presentation of the LEFT BRAIN versus RIGHT BRAIN theory commonly used by neurologist is greatly oversimplified to bring the CORPUS CALLOSUM out of the woods of its tremendous complexity and more into the light of our awareness.

Meanwhile, therapists and researchers from the helping professionals along with neuroscientists will continue to investigate it and to offer us new learning about its amazing ability. What's going to be important to all of us post COVID-19 is our getting up to speed with the CORPUS CALLOSUM as it of necessity becomes even more aware of ourselves not just MINDFULLY and SOULFULLY but both at once. In short, we need to be more aware of ourselves as individuals constantly developing and growing and becoming at-one with the universe PEACEFULLY. A quantum leap forward? Why not?

There is still a large language difference between my world of professional therapists versus that of neuro-biologists. Most of the research related to the brain in my former field of endeavor is from the point of view of the person behind the brain's activity, that is, it is from the point of view of its primary user. It is mostly subjective. Whereas neuro-scientists are mostly objective. In fact, these two modes of learning are not only at the heart of the balancing act going on inside our heads but also are active outside in the world around us. Post COVID-19, we are going to have to bring the persons behind the brain - its users - out into the open by becoming more aware of its enormous power in balancing the four dimensions of our lives - physical and intellectual on the left side of the brain and emotional and spiritual on the right side. What a mix of information and date to be processed. Because of the enormity of this task happening in nanoseconds with and without our awareness and because it all happens interactively, I'm going to suggest that we call the CORPOS CALLOSM something else. I 'm going to suggest that we call it the LOVE LINK. It would be more in the spirit of bringing both sides together and more appropriate to the development of an ongoing SELF-AWARENESS METHODOLOGY.

CHAPTER 4 – LEFT BRAIN, RIGHT BRAIN AND THE GROWING NEED TO BALANCE AND INTEGRATE THE EIGHT SENSES OF THE BODY/BRAIN SYSTEM

As if the discovery of a double-barreled brain with a mixer that processes the two streams of learning into one weren't enough, today's neuro-biologists have discovered much more! In the course of this expansion in the focus of their inquiry, researchers have already learned that in addition to balancing the flow of Left versus Right brain activity, the Corpus Callosum or as I prefer to call it, the Love Link works best when it learns from the bottom up and not from the top down as once thought. And it processes new information in terms of eight senses, not five also as once thought. There are the typical five senses of 1) seeing 2) hearing 3) tasting 4) smell and 5) touching. But there are also three other senses to add to these basic five senses. These are 6) a Sense of Self 7) a Sense of Others and 8) a Sense of "Something Bigger." Hence, we are four dimensional in our outlook on life: physical (Senses 1 to 5), intellectual (Sense 6), emotional (Sense 7) and spiritual (Sense 8).

We need only to observe an infant in action to confirm that these first five senses are most basic to our ongoing development of an information base that gives direction and guidance to us as we related to the world around us. They are, for the most part, physical, that is, they occur in the material realm of our experience and are what we call "real." Entire theories of human behavior are built around them, for example, there are the various therapies based on Behavioral Theory.

The sixth sense – "sense of self" – relates more the intellectual dimension of our lives. For example, there are the various therapies based on Freudian Theory developed by Sigmund Freud nearly 100 years ago. Its version of self-to-world interactions includes an "id" or inner drive system, a "superego" or rules of game as defined by any given society that we find ourselves and an "ego" as intermediary.

The seventh sense – "sense of others" – relates more to the emotional dimension of our lives. For example, there is Jungian Theory. It was developed by Carl Jung, a student of Sigmund Freud. Whereas Freudian Theory is more three dimensional in outlook based on our being attentive to sensations, thoughts and feelings, Jung added a fourth dimension to how we gather information and develop our knowledge and wisdom about the world around. He added intuitions. Because intuitions are more subjective and less objective, Jungian theory is not as accessible to scientific inquiry and even today, less acceptable among professionals. It has however spawned an enormous self-help industry on the industry under the heading of "mindfulness."

Similarly, the eighth sense – what neuro-scientists refer to as "a sense of Something Bigger" – has only more recently found its place among the various professionals formally studying our human interactions with the hope of bettering our human condition. For example, it took Ego Autonomy in the late 1960s and 70s which was the result of a merger of Jungian theory with Freudian theory followed by a cross-referencing of Western thinking with Eastern thinking in the 1980s to open up the minds of theorists to the power of meditation and add the spiritual dimension as legitimate within the scope of their inquiry. In turn, this has made Jung's intuitions a more acceptable focus of their research.

Add to this, the discoveries of quantum physics and the oneness of the vast energy field supports us have propelled us toward the same level of inquiry outwardly in physics and astronomy. Talk about new discoveries. We have eight senses - the usual five that we recognize plus a sixth sense of a sense of ourselves, a seventh sense of a sense of others and an eighth sense of a sense of "something bigger." We have on the one hand, matters of self and the world around us and on the other, matters of soul and cosmos. Individual healing plus soul searching. Plus all that flows between.

We have brains and bodies that work together under our management. Moreover, we have brains that have two hemispheres to give us a four dimensional outlook that is at least double to what it's previously known capacity is. Add to this, we can be open to information not only from five senses but from eight senses! All of which suggests that as individuals, not only do we have a lot to learn but also we have a lot more learning power at our disposal than had previously imagined.

Granted that we have to rethink ourselves as a local and global societies within the context of a cosmic reality. But apparently our basic humanity comes equipped to do it! It just takes a reminder one generation to the next.

Every time we get new pieces of information through our senses, it has to be added to the "gestalt", that is to the "big picture" that we think that we're working on and some other pieces have to be shifted or changed. Some even eliminated. In today's COVID-19 world, it's happening so fast and so unpredictably that is frightening.

On June 5, 2020, I was deeply immersed in the development of my website about the new knowledge and wisdom needed in the post

COVID-19 era when my granddaughter, Monica, almost threw me completely off course with a powerful Facebook reminder of events of the day. She was reacting to the brutal killing of a black man, George Floyd, by a police officer in Minneapolis. The killing was viewed on networked television and read in newspapers by millions of people world- wide. The protests that were resulted had been going on for almost two weeks when she posted her Facebook reminder. I wanted to completely rewrite the opening page of my website about the apparent need for new knowledge combined with wisdom and ongoing discovery to completely review our systems of service delivery...but then I realized that we were in the midst of an ongoing situation. That COVID-19 and our recovery from it along with the new technology would be changing our lives forever. In fact, the post COVID-19 era was already happening. We were already being challenged by so much change and yet it seemed to be happening so slowing. Monica like so many of us was expressing her impatience. She posted a copy of a picture taken of some of our family at a get-together in Winnipeg three years ago along with the following text:

> *"My beautiful multiracial family. I'll be honest, I have been at a loss for what to say, and sometimes feelings of anger and helpless can feel crippling.*

> *"What I want to say is this: Love comes in every color. I don't know how we heal the bad hearts, the broken system, and the hate that can tear us apart. I DO know that all good things from LOVE. Love one another, be kind to one another, support each other, empathize and acknowledge that people have different experiences based solely on the color of their skin. Open eyes, open ears, and open heart. I'd like to say we'll get there some day, get to that place where everyone*

is judged by their action and character, not their exterior. But man, its 2020, when is someday going to come? More important what can we do to get there?" (Monica Goretzky, June 5, 2020, Facebook)

Monica lives with her husband and three children in Katy, Texas, not far from Houston where George Floyd, the most recent victim of racial violence, was buried on June 9, 2020, next to his mother. Naturally, my response as a grandparent was one of great pride. But there was something else. There was a powerful sense of inter-generational connectedness in all of this. I tried address that:

"It has also been my experience that love comes in every color and from every person. However, it does not always find the freedom of expression that it needs to nurture its growth within us. The best thing that any one of us can do, Monica, is what you do so beautifully in you Facebook message, that is, each one of us can keep the love that we are living up-front where we can all see it and enjoy it, enough to learn from one another's experience. The great power of love is that it demonstrates our connectivity with one another and confirms our continuity one generation to the next.

"As you know, I've been a reluctant user of Facebook because I couldn't understand how the new technology would generate a stronger sense of humanity in my life. However, I've changed my mind. Beautifully written. Beautifully lived." (Don Ayre, June 5, 2020, Facebook)

Truly, racism, that is to say, anti-racism, is a major concern one generation to the next. So also is the violence that seems to accompany it. It is one of the changes that must happen. It is crucial to our survival as a humanity that we rid ourselves of both racism and violence. It will take time and dedication. But there is a growing sense of urgency. To sum up in context of Martin Luther King's leadership of what became a global human rights movement:

> *Today our very survival depends on our ability to stay awake, to adjust to new ideas, to remain vigilant and to face the challenges of change. Together we must learn to live as brothers and sisters or we will be forced to perish as fools.* **Martin Luther King Jr., Where Do We Go From Here: Chaos or Community? 1967**

Tragically, it was only a year after he wrote this that Martin Luther King was shot to death in Memphis, Tennessee. But the COVID-19 virus has reawakened his spirit. It is presenting us with yet another opportunity historically for reform and change…if we only can work together as "brothers and sisters" as members of one human family and can continue to build from one generation to the next.

And so it is that my granddaughter has recalled for me my involvement some years ago in the civil rights movements. And the words of Martin Luther King that I would like to bring forward to help us connect yesterday with today and continue our dialogue to make change happen – without violence. But first, let me locate myself and my biases. I am a retired researcher and child and family therapist living at the moment in my sixth week of lock-down in a seniors residence. I was born in Winnipeg, Manitoba in 1935 and followed the line of my education and career development to Family and Children's Services of Pittsburgh where I was project director for a joint study with the University of Pittsburgh. Strange to say that other than fellow students at the University of Manitoba who were from Africa, I had not met a black person prior to moving to Pittsburgh.

Even the research project that I was working on tended to steer away from the obvious issues that prevent people in the black and white cultures especially from working together. Rather, the project was confined to the theories that social work practitioners were using and the consistency of them as therapists as they made professional judgements about the delivery of services. The director of the agency had foreseen computerization and the need for a classification system that we could all relate to as professionals. But there was so much variation from a theoretical point of view - Sigmund Freud versus Carl Jung versus Otto Rank versus Eric Fromm etc. etc. - that it turned out to be a seven year project which I eventually had to complete when I returned to home to teach at the University of Manitoba.

Meanwhile, I had become very caught up with Martin Luther King's civil rights movement and the universality of ourselves as a humanity. When I read and hear today's accusation of American versus Canadian racism, I recall those seven years most vividly. As I saw it, the most basic difference between United States and Canada was that there was a greater reliance on politics to solve the nation's problems and an underlying threat of violence as the ultimate solution in United States. It was an attitude that was a major influence in my returning home to teach.

I had met Jean while we were both working at Family and Children's Services of Pittsburgh but we were married in Winnipeg. The fact is that we probably would not have met were it not for Martin Luther King. It was two years after the Selma, Alabama march and the child and family therapy agency where I worked had just introduced an equal right training program. Jean was amongst those hired. I had been working at the agency for six years having come to Pittsburgh from Canada as a doctoral student and as research director with the agency.

After our initial meeting in the elevator, we started "dating" which meant that we met at Jean's home without ever going out. Although we were both divorced at the time and free to date, it probably would not have been accepted at the agency. In fact, we discovered afterwards that we were illegal in seventeen states so the eventuality of marriage was out of the question in the United States. I decided to return to Winnipeg. I accepted a teaching position at the University of Manitoba where I could continue my research and writing. And we could be married. I taught for seven years before going into private practice where I had even more freedom to follow the lines of inquiry opened up by my research. I retired except for my writing in 1995. We were married and lived with our family in Winnipeg for 50 years.

And so it was that in 2014, I summarized my findings as a researcher and private practitioner in field of child and family therapy. We had just moved out of our home of 46 years to a retirement community. McNally's Bookstore assisted me in its self-publication then made possible through the new technology offered there. I called it *Toward a More Loving and Caring World*. Certainly, it was intent of the therapists that I had worked with through the years and of my own private practice. When I self-published *Toward a More Loving and Caring World* in 2014, I included quotes from various authors including Martin Luther King that had influenced me most profoundly. Now as I read Martin Luther King's words in context of today, I realize that there is much work yet to be done. I share this excerpt with this in mind.

The excerpt from *Toward a More Loving and Caring World* begins here...

When I make the *big connection* of self to stars, it occurs to me that we might not taking very good care of our planet relative to the other ten thousand or so planets out there capable of life like ours; it occurs to me that maybe we need to be taking a less competitive and more cooperative stand nation to nation; it occurs to me that we perhaps should be thinking more in terms of our common human destiny, given the cosmic reality of our lives. There I've said it again: *cosmic reality*. For years, I was shy about mentioning cosmic reality as the context of life and about discussing how the build-up of meditation makes us increasingly aware of it. When I did try to discuss it, people would hum the theme of Rod Sterling's *Twilight Zone* to distract me from my seriousness. But I'm not the only one who is star struck. As Martin Luther King Jr. once said:

> *Something should remind us once more that the great things in this universe are things that we never see. You walk out at night and look up at the beautiful stars as they bedeck the heavens like lanterns of eternity and the think you can see all. Oh, no. You can never see the law of gravitation that hold them there.* **Martin Luther King Jr., Where Do We Go From Here? Chaos or Community? 1967.**

There was the idealism of my religious beliefs and the realism of my academic research that I was having difficulty with… the research that I had started while at Family and Children's Service and wanted to continue while at the University of Pittsburgh and later at the University of Manitoba was regarded as too subjective, too radical. Increasingly, I found myself looking for balance in my brief participation in the civil rights movement and what I knew of the theology of Martin Luther King Jr. His point seemed to have been for people to have the right to express themselves fully, non-violently. I knew him to be a meditator and I began to rely on meditation more myself.

As theology students, Martin Luther King and his wife attended the Unitarian Church in Washington, D.C. He was greatly influenced by the transcendentalists – Emerson, Thoreau, and Margaret Fuller – particularly Thoreau whose writings had influenced Ghandi. As a result, there is strong intergenerational connection between Martin Luther King Jr. and the root thinking not only of the culture predominating the North American continent and but also with the common humanity of all cultures. His civil rights movement is therefore a prime example of *Transformative Meditation* in action:

> *Since being in India, I am more convinced than ever before that the method of nonviolent resistance is the most potent weapon available to oppressed people in their struggle for justice and human dignity. In a real sense, Mahatma Gandhi embodied in his life certain universal principles that are inherent in the moral structure of the universe, and these principles are as inescapable as the law of gravitation.*
> **Martin Luther King Jr., Where Do We Go From Here: Chaos or Community? 1967**

Apparently, we all have within us a positive sense of direction derived from our ongoing development and growth toward fulfillment as individuals and as members of a collective humanity. It is inherent in the moral structure of the Universe. But it is in the form of an ideal that is confronted daily by reality. Not so much an inner commitment As a result, we wrestle in life with the ideal versus the real. If enough of us are exploited and we discover this, we rise up. We've nothing to lose. We participate in a politics of change. Then sometimes the leadership once we have won, turns around an exploits us only differently. The politics of change is tricky. It has to be directed by our collective awareness of our inner divinity and our growing sense of *Universal Love*. This was what Martin Luther King Jr. appealed to…at least, in my experience and to so many others of my generation.

My being drawn to his philosophy years was a natural affinity. Like many of the social activists before him, Martin Luther King Jr. had achieved the knowledge of the all-seeing third eye. Clearly, Martin Luther King Jr. was basically a *Transformative Meditator* who was visionary. However, he was very aware of *meditation* as a total process capable of producing dreams of hope that he could articulate and use to develop as a social movement. He appealed to the inner divinity in all people.

Martin Luther King Jr. had a unique ability to communicate across the broad spectrum of people and connect with enough *Kindred Spirits* to form a movement, not just for the civil rights of Afro-Americans but for the human rights of all global citizens. Given his leadership, we continue to participate globally in a Universal Love that transcends all else. It is a love of humanity as family and in the future of our species; it is a love of one generation for the next. Meditation has this transforming power in that it helps us to recognize that life is a puzzle that has no borders and no end in sight…only ongoing mystery. It is ours for the making. It is for our inner peace to find outer harmony. As Martin Luther King put it:

> One of the great liabilities of history is that all too many people fail to remain awake though great periods of social change. Every society has its protector of the status quo

and its fraternities of the indifferent who are notorious for sleeping through revolutions. But today our very survival depends on our ability to stay awake, to adjust to new ideas, to remain vigilant and to face the challenges of change. Together we must learn to live as brothers and sisters or we will be forced to perish as fools.

We must work passionately and indefatigably to bridge the gulf between our scientific progress and or moral progress. One of the great problems of humankind is that we suffer from a poverty of the spirit which stands in glaring contrast to our scientific and technological abundance. The richer we have become materially, the poorer we have become morally and spiritually….so much of modern life can be summarized in that suggestive phrase by Thoreau: Improved means to an unimproved end. **Martin Luther King, Where Do We Go From Here? 1968.**

The excerpt *from Toward a More Loving and Caring World* ends here…

Given what I had written and self-published in 2014, it was therefore with delight – no other word for it – that I read Monica's post on Facebook. It was a powerful reminder one generation to the next. But it added something. Urgency!

In fact, that's what the COVID-19 virus was adding. Urgency. For some time now, the whole world has been struggling to survive the COVID-19 crisis physically. And rightly so. But the crisis is also impacting on our lives mentally, emotionally and spiritually. And other issues are surfacing. The gradual resolution of the current crises will not end until we address all four dimensions of its world-wide attack on us. Moreover, the COVID-19 crisis has reminded us yet again that our systems locally through to nationally and globally are not perfect. The relentless pressure that it has been putting on us has surfaced yet another series of systemic shortfalls, this time related to our delivery of justice itself. It has exposed our racism!

Add to this, the COVID-19 crisis has divided our attention and our energy for reform. "Stay at home, protect others." "Get out and demonstrate." But in either case, it means to make change happen. The post COVID-19 era of reformation has started. In the immediate sense, it seems conflicting but over the long haul of the growth and human development that has been going on one generation to the next, it is definitely doable. But it will take the integration of the four dimensions of life – physical, mental, emotional and spiritual – within ourselves as individuals. And in some cases, this will mean a major adjustment of our world view and a complete rethinking of the world around us. Even so, change has to happen and quickly. The pain of not changing is too much.

I've already said it: It will take a more balanced dialogue among one another and one generation to the next. It will take new knowledge and new wisdom: New and increasingly enlightened leaning and thinking, new and increasingly enlightened theories and ideas, new and increasingly enlightened assumptions and feelings, and even new and increasingly enlightened philosophies and beliefs. Above all, new and increasingly enlightened discoveries and action. It can't be said enough: New and increasingly enlightened knowledge combined with new and increasingly enlightened wisdom is the key to our working together toward a more loving and caring tomorrow. My hope in recalling the words and leadership of Martin Luther King, I will have added to my granddaughter's powerful Facebook reminder in a way that will move us yet another notch.

But then I was drawn back to some thing in my own words six years ago. Apparently back then when I was reviewing my practice as a family and child therapist, I had said: *"When I make the big connection of self to stars, it occurs to me that we might not taking very good care of our planet relative to the other ten thousand or so planets out there capable of life like ours; it occurs to me that maybe we need to be taking a less competitive and more cooperative stand nation to nation; it occurs to me that we perhaps should be thinking more in terms of our common human destiny, given the cosmic reality of our lives. There I've said it again: cosmic reality. For years, I was shy about mentioning cosmic reality as the context of life and about discussing how the build-up of meditation makes us increasingly aware of it. When I did try to discuss it, people would hum the theme of Rod Sterling's Twilight Zone to distract me from my seriousness."*

Then I was pleased to have discovered that I'm not the only one who was star struck. As Martin Luther King Jr. once said:

> *"Something should remind us once more that the great things in this universe are things that we never see. You walk out at night and look up at the beautiful stars as they bedeck the heavens like lanterns of eternity and the think you can see all. Oh, no. You can never see the law of gravitation that hold them there.* **Martin Luther King Jr., Where Do We Go From Here? Chaos or Community? 1967.***"*

Exactly. For some reason, we are reluctant to stretch our minds to the full extent of their present awareness. We need "stepping stones" to help us along, even on our cosmic journeying.

But why we are so shy about our experiences of what's "beyond' today. Beyond even the "here and now"? We do we resist visions of a "cosmic reality?" Why are we so shy about our present experiences of reality even locally and globally? Is it that we don't feel equipped to deal with it?

More recent readings of microbiological researchers as well as in my own field of psycho-social development suggest that we not only have two hemispheres cold use cooperatively rather than competitively in the processing of information but we have eight senses not five that we can use to get information about the world around us. And that is the "stuff" of a four dimensional outlook on life - material, intellectual, emotional and spiritual.

What it gets down to is this: We are apparently equipped with the makings of a four dimensional lens to put together our perceptions of life but we don't necessarily develop, and we don't necessary use the full extent of our four-fold intelligence with its contestant tendency to grow and change when we make our decision about life! We like to see ourselves as integrated or "whole" person but not necessarily others, not necessarily society and for sure, not necessary humanity. So we are frustrated. We live in a three dimensional world of our own making but increasingly, we are becoming aware of ourselves as four dimensional creatures. We created race as means of thinking about life but it conflicts with our growing sense of humanity and needs to be rooted out and replaced with a new sense of ourselves and our global community.

CHAPTER 5 – EXAMPLES OF STEPPING STONES FOR ONGOING GROWTH AND DEVELOPMENT

We are constantly trying to find new ways for self-healing and soul-searching. It's a basic inner conversation left-brain to right brain. Moreover, we are trying to find new ways to convert our applying what we come up with to our advantage. It's a matter of converting methodology into strategy. Our personal interests become political. It's what we might call satisfying our inner sense of growth and development - indeed, our sense of PROGRESS. Without it, life has no hope.

And so while this is the fourth of the SELF-AWARENESS PAPERS, I expect there will be many more. It is clearly based on the formula MINDFULNESS and SOULFULNESS to PEACEFULNESS but adds something else - a stronger sense of PROGRESS. Hopefully others who find this website will be prompted to contribute their thinking. But for sure, I will be continuing to post my discoveries. It seems that the brain needs four elements to be rational (physical and intellectual) and humane (emotional and spiritual) in its decision making and its growth and development - open-mind balance, integration, progress This is the fourth progress position paper related to the fourth. I invite comments about progress.

However, it seems that the four papers thus far have found themselves in order of development as chapters of a book. This can happen. But it was the result largely of my granddaughter interrupting me in the development of a website about the importance today of new and increasingly enlightened knowledge and wisdom. "New Discoveries" I called my position papers initially. Then it dawned on me that it is urgent that they happen, perhaps in a self-published book. That somehow they may be a part of a tsunami of personal and political information that is much-needed to make the next step forward in civilization. Strange to think that one's point of view is what important. But why else the need for protests. But why else the need for leadership that listens.

I tried self-publishing for the first time in the 60s. It was not easy back then. I had worked as a researcher for Family and Children's Services of Pittsburgh for six years on a special project aimed at finding a common language among the thirty or so therapist who worked there, all from different academic backgrounds. It was a theory building project conducted jointly with the University of Pittsburgh. It anticipated that computers were on the horizon of the administration family service agencies and that a universal classification system would be a necessity. I was still working on it when I left to teach in my home community, Winnipeg.

The arrangement with the School of Social Work there at the University of Manitoba was that I would continue my research while I taught. Publish or perish is the imperative of career development for academics. But there was no University Press at the University of Manitoba there so I had to use a grant to pay for publication by a private printer. What I didn't realize, however, is that control over the printed word and the distribution of knowledge was very strict back then. That's where I first learned about the distinction between knowledge and wisdom and the division of the two steams of learning.

Regardless, I self-published two manuscripts to share with my students: 1) New Hope for Old Ways and 2) Love Within Limits. I distributed it by hand to the students. Both expressed the practices of the workers at Family and Children's Services of Pittsburgh, but were not acceptable to the School of Social Work because they introduced "unproven theories," namely The Art of Loving by Eric Fromm, The Broken Image by Floyd Matson and, going back even further, Modern Man In Search of a Soul by C.G. Jung. However, the school had built its acceptance with the academic community as Freudian-based and did not want to risk being "unscientific."

Later the computer arrived and it was much easier to type and run off book-like copies of manuscripts. Eventually the internet was discovered and previously academically-controlled books could not only be published but distributed off-campus. Moreover, it was possible to become a one person office. As a result, I went into private practice. TOWARD A MORE LOVING AND CARING WORLD was a culmination of all of my ongoing research writings to that date, 2005. In every sense of the word, it was the result of a work in progress. I had self-published five times in between my efforts at the University of Manitoba and 2005.

Shortly after the book launch of TOWARD A MORE LOVING AND CARING WORLD, I asked the staff of McNally's Booksellers to experiment a little with the location of my book in their store by trying it out in different genres. They had located it in the *Psychology Section* of the bookstore prior to the launch but from the responses to it in the question and answer period at the launch, I had become convinced that it was not viewed that way or, at least, not exclusively. Clearly, it was also viewed as theology – a combination of both psychology and theology. There might be a better book-shelf neighborhood for it where potential buyers – "kindred spirits," I had called them – would find it more easily. But where?

At first, we tried the *Metaphysics Section*; then the *New Age Section*. Eventually, we settled on the *Spiritual Teaching Section* as a good neighborhood to be visible in and to use as a base for ongoing inquiry. So we tried it for about a month. Just above it was a shelf called *Mindfulness*. Curious, I glanced through the pages of the books on the *Mindfulness Section* and selected a few to take home for closer scrutiny. I'm a reader who likes to write in the margins of books so libraries don't find my reading habits too acceptable.

As I pieced together what I could of *Mindfulness*, I began to solve a mystery that had been nagging in the back of my mind ever since I completed the manuscript for TOWARD A MORE LOVING AND CARING WORLD. Back when I had chosen to leave the University to develop my private practice as a family and child therapist and to continue my research without being restricted, it was mostly because of the new director of the School of Social Work preferred what he called "the science of social engineering" as compared with "the art of individual therapy." His approach, he insisted, was more politically valid and objective; mine, was more personally directed and subjective.

A SUBJECTIVE METHODOLOGY

In particular, I wanted to combine psychology and sociology with an element of spirituality and I wanted to introduce meditation as a methodology toward this end. At about the same time on other North American campuses, other therapists were being influenced by Pierre De Chardin, Carl Jung, Eric Fromm, and Alan Watts. Later, it was Maharishi, Ken Wilbur, Dali Lama, Deepak Chopra...all of whom have added to my thinking over the years. There were more writers that I considered to be great minds, of course. But the mystery that continued to nag at me was: What had happened to their influence in particular on others in my profession? Had these great minds managed to change campus thought at other Universities teaching child and family therapy? I didn't know for sure. I had been working too independently. Certainly, the Internet had served as a platform for an abundance of self-help books written by academics and therapist.

It turns out that they had set the climate for the formation of a new and revolutionary movement in departments of psychology and sociology on many campuses and among many of their graduating therapists called MINDFULNESS. Based on a blending of Eastern philosophy with Western thinking, it is a combination of psychological and spiritual concepts that regards meditation as central to our mental health and to our decision making in all areas of life. Moreover, it is entirely appropriate for the development within individuals for today's much-needed global mindset. Not surprisingly, Jung's coveted Red Book is well-known to the MINDFULNESS movement. And of course, to Buddhist practitioners.

Initially, I was quite excited as I read through the books in the *Mindfulness Section*. I thought: Aha, here's where the threads of progress had been picked up and interwoven into a new psychology guiding therapists and self-development enthusiasts. But as I read through the other books on the shelf designated "Mindfulness," I realized that the research in my book was less technical, more spiritual. From my experience as a family and child therapist, I had concluded it was not enough to merge Freudian and Jungian theories with Buddhist meditation in particular. There had to be a stronger element of spirituality – call it *"soulfulness"* – to balance our scientific learning with our spiritual awareness.

OBJECTIVE EXPERIENCE

Clearly, my professional experience as outlined in my earlier writing of TOWARD A MORE LOVING AND CARING WORLD had been somewhere between Spiritual Teaching shelf and the Mindfulness shelf. Jung's writings and Fromm's four kinds of love were useful to me in making sense out of my practice. As I searched further, I found that it's not just psychology that's been advancing. Theology has also become less defined by religious doctrine and more by individual experiences of spirituality. It's known as *Soulfulness*. Meditation is the common ground between the two where we are at peace and the mind is open to the soul. As David Benner puts it:

Meditation is a doorway to our center. Or, using more psychological knowledge, meditation opens the possibility of accessing our unconscious and, therefore, to living with a stronger alliance between the conscious and the unconscious dimensions of our being. Meditation is a path from ordinary awareness to spiritual awareness, from a knowing about things to a knowing of them. This means that meditation is far more than a way of trying to still ourselves. It is a way of opening our self so that we can be found by our center – by the spirit of God – and therein truly find our self. From Spirituality and the Awakening Self by David Brenner.

TRENDS IN MINDFULNESS and SOULFULNESS

So there is today on the one hand, *"mindfulness"*; and on the other, *"soulfulness."* Further research is needed to learn how these revolutionary new trends in psychology and theology respectively are useful to us in linking together SELF with SOUL within each one of us. *Mindfulness* relates to what I had been calling "developing the SELF;" *Soulfulness* relates to "growing the SOUL." By using meditation along with readings from great minds who have gone generations before us we wake up our common sense of humanity and optimism. By integrating MINDFULNESS with SOULFULNESS, we can create within ourselves a more holistic sense of SELF and a wholeness of worldview that is more loving and caring.

The Internet, I have found, is alive with ongoing research and practical how-to information on both subjects and for linking the two. It's a matter, it seems, of our being open to life's four most basic questions: Who am I? What's life all about? Where do I fit in? and Why are we here? It's a matter of being both objective and subjective in our lines of inquiry.

I never did find a section in McNally's Bookstore that was totally comfortable to me as a location to display my book TOWARD A MORE LOVING AND CARING WORLD. But I did find two more books to add to my library at home…I like to think of them now as the first two stepping stones toward new knowledge as I rewrite this website as applicable to today's COVID-19 pandemic. Based on my earlier research regarding life's four most basic questions, I anticipated that I would need two additional writings to round off these first two books.

An EXAMPLE of a STEPPING STONE for GROWTH #1 - CHANGE

THE BRAIN THAT CHANGES ITSELF: STORIES OF PERSONAL TRIUMPH FROM THE FRONTIERS OF BRAIN SCIENCE by Norman Doidge (Penguin Books 2007).

M.D. Doidge is a psychiatrist, psychoanalyst and researcher working out of Columbia University and the University of Toronto. Doidge and his associates change the way we understanding ourselves… radically. We don't have one brain working for us. We have two: a Left Hemisphere that is rational and logical in all that it does and quite rigid about it; and a Right Hemisphere that is intuitive and open minded. Amazingly, the two brains are able to get along and make decisions about life that are workable...or not. As a result, the brain is constantly engaged in an inner dialogue and is growing and developing to meet life's challenges. All of this happens in nanosecond and beyond our awareness...unless we work at it. It's up to us. Plasticity, it's called. The brain is constantly growing and changing...as much as we will allow.

The writer of the preface of his book explains: "Doidge writes about the new and revolutionary discovery that the human brain can change itself, as told through the stories of the scientists, doctors, and patients who have together brought about astonishing transformations. Without operations or medications, they have made use of the brain's hitherto unknown ability to change. His book paints a complete picture of the importance of altruism and the world's need for it, and explores its impact in society, politics, the economy, the environment, and education."

The New York Times in its review goes even further in its hope for change prompted by Doidge: "In bookstores, the science aisle generally lies well away from the self-help section, with hard reality on one set of shelves and wishful thinking on the other. But Norman Doidge fascinating synopsis of the current revolution in neuroscience straddles this gap: the age-old distinction between the brain and the mind is crumbling fast as the power of positive thinking finally gains scientific credibility. Mind-bending, miracle-working, reality-busting stuff with implications...not only individual patients with neurological diseases but for all human beings, not to mention human culture, human learning and human history."

I set aside THE BRAIN THAT CHANGES ITSELF as the first STEPPING STONE for our ongoing inquiry relevant to the challenge of COVID-19 virus because its author, Norman Doidge, M.D. clearly demonstrates that our brains are equipped to the enormous growth that is going to be required of us. It's very reassuring to know this.

An EXAMPLE of a STEPPING STONE for GROWTH #2 - COMPASSION

ALTRUISM: THE POWER OF COMPASSION TO CHANGE YOURSELF AND THE WORLD by Matthieu Ricard (Little, Brown and Company, 2015).

Matthieu Ricard is a Buddhist priest, well known internationally for his workshop and lectures. In his book Altruism, he demonstrates from a review of the research happening worldwide that Altruism is a common human need in that if the world we are living in doesn't provide the opportunity for it, we don't grow and develop in terms of our humanity. More importantly, we don't experience happiness. So we not only look for opportunities to be altruistic, we create them.

A review on the Internet, explains: "Entrepreneurs, economists, and thinkers have embraced Ricard's message. In over 800 pages of research, he provides scientific evidence that we aren't selfish human beings driven only by our own interests. Moreover, today's society is not more violent than it was in the past. Yes, we can change the way we are and, therefore, cooperate more, not only on an individual level, but on a community level, too. Whether it is related to economy, environment, our well-being, or our relationships with others, we will all benefit from accepting and developing altruism. This idea is not supported only by the monk, but also by science. It's called Evolutionism. Neurology, psychology, as well as case studies on conflicts, all show that altruism is not only a behavior inborn in people, but it can also be developed. To become a better person is really something possible, as long as we accept some obvious facts that we have forgotten. It will appeal to anyone and everyone who seeks to create a more positive and sustainable future."

I set aside ALTRUISM as the SECOND STEPPING STONE that we will need to meet the challenge of COVID-19. The first STEPPING STONE is about SELF and the SECOND STEPPING STONE is about WORLD. That was five years ago in McNally's Book Store that I chose those two books, the one representative of the SELF-side of my MINDFULNESS and the other representative of the WORLD-side of my MINDFULNESS. I suppose that one could say that it was the LEFT BRAIN and the RIGHT BRAIN working together to achieve a balance through my selection of food for thought! But I have only a beginning awareness of how the CORPOS CALLOSUM works in the regard. But it fascinates me. Besides there was my SOUFULNESS to work into the mix.

As I read through these two books, I knew from experience that it would not be enough. As a researcher, I needed to have at least four books on the go at once. Some sort of cross-fertilization process, I suppose. However, I'm still hoping to discover why other than it's an old research habit. It was like having four cornerstones in place to give direction to my ongoing learning. No. Not cornerstones. That would box my learning in and never wanted that. More like stepping stones. I find that I am always reaching out for new learning. Assigning myself new projects as needed and nurturing them by searching for relevant ideas rather than building them.

Nonetheless as it so often happens, I went back to the shelves of books in McNally's Bookstore and found two more books to compliment Stepping Stone #1: The Brain that Changes Itself and

Stepping Stone #2: Altruism and round off my knowledge base for the revision of my website relevant to COVID-19 pandemic. These two books are just typical of what's going to be needed by way of our expanded notions of MINDFULNESS 1) a growing and changing brain 2) a solid sense of togetherness.

An EXAMPLE of a STEPPING STONE for GROWTH #3 - MINDFULNESS

THE MINDFUL BRAIN: REFLECTIONS AND ATTUNEMENT IN THE CULTIVATION OF WELL-BEING by Daniel Siegel (W.W. NORTON COMPANY 2007).

The notes on the dust cover begin by noting that "Mindfulness is by no means a new fad." Then it goes on to explain: "Ancient cultures and religions worldwide have long drawn on various methods, from medication and prayer and tai-chi, to help individuals move toward well-being by focusing their attention and attuning to the present. Now, mindful awareness has been scientifically proven to enhance our physical, mental and social well-being. With this empirical evidence in hand, Siegel embarks on a ground breaking approach to integrate findings from cutting-edge research with the wisdom and of mindfulness practice demonstrate how this learning skill may actually work, and how its cultivation can enrich our lives."

This book pushes the thinking of Norman Doidge toward SOULFULNESS and it is fascinating to read to read the two of them in tandem. Whereas Doidge discusses SELF in the context of WORLD, Seigel discusses SOUL in the context of COSMOS thus establishing two lines of inquiry consistent with there being a left hemisphere and a right hemisphere to our brains. I'm stretching the meaning of both authors, I'm sure. But why not? We're using the findings of their research as STEPPING STONES, after all.

An EXAMPLE of a STEPPING STONE for GROWTH #4 - ENERGY

The FIELD: The Quest for the Secret Force of the UNIVERSE by Lynne McTaggart (HarperCollins Publishers 2008)

Again we look to the covers of books like this before we begin flipping through the pages and then settle in to learn what we can. On the back cover of the field, the publishers says: "*In this ground breaking classic, investigative journalist reveals a radical new paradigm - that the human mind and body are not separate from the environment but a packet of pulsating power constantly interacting with this vast energy sea, and that conspicuousness may be central in shaping our world. The Field is a highly readable scientific story presenting a stunning picture of an interconnected universe and a new scientific theory that makes sense of supernatural phenomena.*" The fact is that we are gifted with both a body and a brain at birth but with unlimited growth relative to the vast universe in which we find ourselves. It depends on us.

For simplicity's sake, I have avoided quoting from any of the STEPPING STONES. What's important is that these four researcher-authors and others like them are exploring new territory and pointing out discoveries along the way that are both MINDFUL and SOULFUL beyond belief. Like the previous three authors cited as STEPPING STONE researchers, Lynne McTaggart documents the work of a new breed of scientists who are exploring the energy field of which we are a part and parcel. It is a matter of catching up our thinking as a whole with the work of quantum physics.

She concludes from a review of their work: "There need no longer be two truths, the truth of science and the truth of religion. There could be one unified vision of the world."

An EXAMPLE of STEPPING STONES for GROWTH #5 - EXPERIENCE

MY STROKE OF INSIGHT: A BRAIN SCIENTIST'S PERSONAL JOURNEY by Jill Bolte Taylor Ph. D. (Penguin Books 2009).

We all like to read about one another's experiences by way of authenticity. This is particularly true of life-changing events that happen to us along the way of the aging process but for Jill Bolte Taylor, the life-changing event that impact her life most significantly happened earlier than expected. She was a 37 year old Harvard trained scientist when she experienced a massive stroke in the left hemisphere below her brain. Amazingly, she was able to experience herself having a stroke and to seek help. More than that, in her eight year recovery period, she was able to record her experience in a way that has help others recognize early system and with the recovery she not only had been studying but experienced!

HOW WE READ AND INFORM OURSELVES

I mention these five books as possible cornerstones setting the parameters of inquiry for this websites - as a base but not a box. More as stepping stones, I suppose. 1) The position that Doidge takes in his book, The Brain That Changes Itself, is that as a major participant in the physical dimension of our lives, the brain is always growing and changing. 2) In his book, Altruism, Ricard points out that we best grow and change through the power of compassion expressed in the context of altruism. 3) In his book, The Mindful Brain, Seigel expands the newly discovered notion of "mindfulness" to be at least three dimensional in the overall sense of wisdom that it brings to our lives - physical, intellectual and emotional. 4) In the book, The Field, Lynne McTaggart reminds us of the spiritual dimension of our lives and of the unknown of the yet-to-be-discovered. 5) My Stroke of Insight: A Brain Scientist's Personal Journey by Jill Bolte Taylor, Ph. D.

These five "stepping stones" and others like them will have set the parameters of the inquiry of this book, not by boxing us in but by giving us the reassurance that we need to venture out from the known to the unknown. Together, I submit, they represent the extent of our present cosmic consciousness, individually and collectively. Granted they are ten years old at the time of this writing. We should be constantly reviewing our stepping stones and for balance and integration as well as for the direction in which they are leading us. And we should be open to change. Even to replacement. My walk through McNally's Bookstore five years ago with my self-published book in hand was exactly that kind experience for me.

So now I ask myself: "Where do we look now to build our futures? How do we turn our brains loose to feed itself while at the same time managing and giving direction to it? I never was a good library user. Even when I was attending a university. I write in the margins of books and like have them at home where I can visit over and over. So I used to shop for food thought more at the likes of McNally's Bookstore than elsewhere. Mostly because stores like McNally's understand readers like me. We like to be comfortable as we wander from shelf to shelf and we like to read as we go. But eventually we do buy. We're collectors, after all. It just takes gentle persuasion. Not only that, there are in bookstores like McNally's massive rack of magazines to keep us current.

And now add to this, there is the Internet. My library of eBooks is large and growing. And there is also the immediacy of "googling" for information.

So I didn't find a permanent shelf for my book, Toward a More Loving and Caring World, but typically I did add two more written by "kindred spirits." And one book led to another. I found two more books and I added them to my home library to help me put form to my ongoing learning experiences and build the basic compendium of information for this website, in particular. It's the way we feed our brains.

But something else happened. I also manage to make my book available on amazon.ca and maybe that's where it belongs. Like this website, it's a work in progress, ever-changing and open to dialogue. So how we find our food for thought has changed - as with all things, radically. Like everyone else, I now search for books on the Internet and buy books electronically. And yes, I have a library of eBooks.

It's a very different way of reading and writing for a very different world of readers and writers. It's somehow being built on top of the zillions of books being stored in libraries and made available in book stores around the world. Like the awareness of our brain has a remarkable two hemisphere organ, the internet is just a little more than twenty years old! Think about how much has changed since the computer came into our lives. For our grandchildren and for our great grandchildren. Like any new discovery, it's not just an add-on. It pushes our brains to grow to keep pace. It's already revolutionizing the way we are educating ourselves and our children. It's only just begun.

First it was the printing press that revolutionized by making the thoughts of great minds accessible to the ordinary person. That was only 300 years ago. Then it was television that revolutionized our book-learning ways. It was the beginning of what we called an information age. It brought information from the world stage into our living rooms. Remember. That was only 70 years ago. Now it's the computer and the Internet! It's whole new ways of learning about ourselves and the universe piled on top of another. It's becoming more and more difficult to makes sense out of it all! MINDFULNESS plus SOULFULNESS equals PEACEFULNESS is a working formula that we can use to balances and rebalance our lives and to integrate the fast flow of information in ways that lets us participate in and contribute to the building of a more loving and caring world, person to person and one generation to the next.

CHAPTER 6 - AGING MINDFULLY, SOULFULLY AND PEACEFULLY

Aging is a Lifelong Process. I'm very aware of this even though I'm 85 now and living in a retirement community where I am pretty much sheltered from the ravages and ongoing suffering caused by COVID-19. My residence is well-managed and safe. For the past six months or so, we have been in "lockdown" meaning that no visitors unless essential for home care, meals served in our rooms and of course masks when we walk the halls or attend exercise and other recreational activities offered in the halls with the proviso that we wear masks and are at six feet distance from one another. There are 125 residents in our community, most of us a long ways past retirement age of 65 and preoccupied with health issues related to our age. Needless to say, we are in complete agreement with the restrictions, not only for personal safety but also for the protection of others – specifically residents, staff and care workers. But we miss seeing one another in dining room, at the mailboxes and in the halls. We miss the opportunities that we once had to SMILE. But that makes one another even more important.

We will have to be increasingly aware of ourselves and the world around us four dimensionally. And we will have to rethink ourselves from the bottom up as individuals within a humanity before we can do that. All of us, young and old, will have to seek new ways of aligning ourselves with our humanity and integrating our living. In short, we will have to revise our collective thinking upwards from its present 3D to a 4D outlook. Or else we will continue to build a worldwide society that is open to pandemics of other names. We tend to think "body, mind and spirit" whereas we are "body, mind, heart and spirit." We are going to have to change. But to do that, we are going to have to know more about ourselves and our common human destiny. We are going to have to align ourselves personally and politically with our cosmic reality. Are we ready for it?

It's not surprising that scientists and academics who are free thinking have been constantly researching and advancing the knowledge base guiding our socioeconomic development under the headings of MINDFULNESS in the direction of a more loving global community; and SOULFULNESS in the direction of a more caring alignment with the universe whole. But their findings have been kept in the background of the knowledge and wisdom directing our personal and political lives. Instead, the dreaded CODVID-19 virus has caught us between two personal and political extremes: to mask or not to mask. Both sides are arguing that it is a matter of freedom of choice. Whereas science has advanced our thinking about our human nature.

In the fields of neurology and biology, for example, researchers have confirmed five major discoveries about how our brain's work on our behalf and how they help us build notions of our SELVES and the WORLD around us that lead to balanced and integrated points of view. The new platform of learning that has developed is being used by clinicians in the field of medicine to do some amazing things with patients who have had strokes, for example. But it goes even further. It is already revolutionizing how we work together globally by combining with our previous psychosocial notions and today's technology to create entirely new approaches to self-help.

Similarly in the field of neurochemistry, there is research that is useful clinically and that advances our knowledge and wisdom of ourselves. And on and on in other fields of study. The problem is our connectivity versus our generativity. If we linger too long in the connectivity of life, we lose track of the depth of it one generation to the next. If we linger too long in the continuity of life, we lose track of the breadth and intensity of the moment. We need to experience life as in integrated and balanced whole. We need an integrated and balanced outlook on life including its physical, intellectual, emotional, spiritual dimensions….For now, COVID-19 has us fixated on the physical and intellectual dimensions.

New Learning for a New Post Pandemic Era

1) Todays learning suggests ways in which we can deal with the mass of learning that is coming our way as a global community faced with something entirely new to us – COVID-19. It gives new confidence to the two major streams of learning recognized as MINDFULNESS and SOULFULNESS. Together these two learning streams twist and turn throughout our lives toward a PEACEFULNESS that confirms moments of balance and integration of left and right hemisphere and SELF to WORLD.

2) For starters, we are in need of rethinking about our personal and political lives – SELF on the one side and WORLD on the other - in major ways. We need to think more holistically. Thus far, we had been going about life with the four dimensions of our living – physical, intellectual, emotional and spiritual - separate and apart from one another whereas holistically means they should be integrated and balanced as one. It is the very basis of an ecological perspective and how we are connected not only with one another but also one generation to the next. Flash forward

to today, COVID-19 becomes just another issue confronting us as we advance ourselves as a species - like global warming, for example.

3) Since the 1980s, neuroscientists using today's technology to study have discovered that we have an organic awareness of ourselves and the world around us and in particular of the plasticity of the Brain as well as the Body in service of our personal and political growth and development. The brain is not a computer. It is a growing and changing organ. This plasticity enables our ongoing growth and development as humans by expanding our world view four dimensionally – conscious or not. All four dimensions - physical, intellectual, emotional and spiritual are in fact our reality. Anything less is problematic. A 4D outlook properly balanced and integrated opens us up to glimpses of the future that we are building!

4) Following up on their studies of the brain's holistic outlook, neuroscientists have also learned that we have a developmental awareness of not only of the five basic senses that gather information for the brain but also we have an additional three sense for a total of eight senses. There are the well-known five senses of 1) Seeing 2) Hearing 3) Smelling 4) Tasting and 5) Touching plus there are three additional senses of 6) Sense of SELF 7) Sense of Others 8) Sense of "Something Bigger." A sense of OTHER is what we are struggling with at the present. The first seven senses are presently being studied as MINDFULNESS by way of techniques to achieve this very important goal. The eight sense of "SOMETHING BIGGER" is allocated to a separate level of study called SOULFULNESS. Ideally, all eight senses are balanced and integrated as one.

5) Neuroscientists have also confirmed that we have an ever-expanding awareness of how the two hemispheres of the brain, Left and Right, process information four dimensionally and give ongoing and accumulative guidance to our interactions with the world around us – mostly physical and intellectual from the left and emotional and spiritual from the right. Hence there is an ongoing dialogue within our SELVES that contributes not only to our personal and social functioning but also to our political well-being and common good. Most important, the brain processes new information from the bottom up and not the top down.

6) Finally (for now) scientists and academics in neurobiology and researches in other fields of study have confirmed that we have an ever-growing awareness of how the two hemispheres of the brain, Left and Right, combine their two streams of learning into a single operational model that is physical, intellectual, emotional and spiritual and thereby four dimensional based on the SELF and WORLD that we build cooperatively or competitively for ourselves. Other scientists and clinicians have advanced this learning and recognized that there are two streams of learning, MINDFULNESS on the one hand and SOULFULNESS on the other. In between the Left and Right brain is the Corpus Callosum ever-reaching toward PEACEFULNESS.

Adding these new insights to what we already have been learning about our growth and development in other fields of study, scientists and academics have been able to pool their knowledge and glimpse the future. New studies are ongoing and with the aid of a technology that has grown far beyond the original insights of the Apple IIe computer and its potential as a word processing, spreadsheet and data base machine. We now have the interconnectivity of an Internet! We are discovering, for example, that the structure of the universe and its galaxies is comparable to that of a human brain and its neurotransmitters. In other words, we have to rethink our notion of SELF and WORLD to include an ever-expanding and deeper sense of SELF and a wider sense of WORLD. MINDFULNESS and SOULFULNESS become two interactive spheres of learning. Change is happening. Are we ready for it? Are we ready to think four dimensionally, that is, through the four lenses of experience – Physical, Intellectual, Emotional, and Spiritual? Personally, perhaps. But politically? We are after all becoming a global community by force of COVID-19.

In fact, all of our systems from health through to education may have to be reviewed and realigned relevant the way we view ourselves and the world around us. The brain is not a machine nor even a computer as we once viewed it. It is a living organism open to change as it processes information and guides our interactions. We are the world that we are building.

Most professionals in the fields of human growth and development agree. Moreover, they are intrigued by something the likes of what they are calling the CORPUS CALLOSUM that balances and integrates our learning from these two streams. It ensures that both sides of the brain can communicate and send signals to each other to converge the two streams of learning, MINDFULNESS to SOULFULNESS, into one.

In fact, what therapists of most persuasions do in the course of their practice is to position themselves as a sort of trusted friend to an overworked and confused CORPUS CALLOSUM and enter into the left hemisphere to right hemisphere conversations that are constantly going on within us. By their feedback, they help us to slow things down and to better sort and align the flow of information coming at us second by second. This ongoing processing can also be enhanced by way of self-help.

But what is truly amazing about the CORPUS CALLOSUM in particular is that it goes about its work regardless of our management of it, that is, regardless of whether we are fully at the helm or not. It somehow accepts and understands that its primary job is to balance and integrate the learning of the left hemisphere (physical and intellectual dimensions) and right hemisphere (emotional and spiritual dimensions). In doing so, it automatically brings a 4D outlook into play by coordinating a resolution of the differences of amongst the four dimensions. Thus, we are constantly balancing and integrating of our learning relative to our growth and development by way of the brain's plasticity and our basic human integrity. This accounts for the inner dialogue that goes on within us. It's a matter of how aware we are of our basic humanity.

The second job of the CORPUS CALLOSUM is to participate in and contribute to the building of a reality that is balanced and integrated. It builds what it thinks. In this way, it is responsible for how we act in terms of our connectivity with one another and our continuity one generation to the next. Thus we are both personal and political in our interactions as we go through life. Love's connectivity roughly translated is our MINDFULNESS stream of learning – all that's physical and intellectual pasted together interactively by what we call our OBJECTIVITY, that is, allowable emotions. Love's continuity roughly translated is our SOULFULNESS stream of learning – all that emotional and spiritual pasted together interactively by what we call our SUBJECTIVITY, that is, allowable intuitions.

The proportionality and mix of MINDFULNESS learning and SOULFULNESS learning varies from person to person depending on life perspective each one of us has. Regardless, we all seek the same thing – a PEACEFULNESS that we know as LOVE. What the CORPUS CALLOSUM does if we let it, is truly awesome!

4. Giving Voice to Aging Mindfully, Soulfully and Peacefully

Thus the PEACEFULNESS that we experience as ideals and values is confirmed by how we live our lives and find expression for the humanity-within us. And we participate in and contribute to the world around us accordingly. What is personal becomes political. Strangely enough, aging is a time in our lives when we can step back from our lives and look at our SELVES and the WORLD around us...and wonder.

BEYOND MINDFULNESS and SOULFULNESS is a PEACEFULNESS called LOVE. In a New Post-Pandemic Era, AGING will be more focused on learning to live peacefully as one, balanced and integrated and on learning to live as a Humanity with a common awareness of destiny. Most important, it will be possible for aging people to participate in and contribute to the social and economic development of our communities worldwide. It will be possible for us at all levels of the aging process to accept and to be guided by the immense sense of WONDER that presently lies sleeping within us., particularly as the voice of the aging gathers in numbers and is stronger.

FROM GOOGLE:

"The world's population is ageing: virtually every country in the world is experiencing growth in the number and proportion of older persons in their population.

Population ageing is poised to become one of the most significant social transformations of the twenty-first century, with implications for nearly all sectors of society, including labor and financial markets, the demand for goods and services, such as housing, transportation and social protection, as well as family structures and intergenerational ties."

Older persons increasingly see themselves as active participants in and contributors to the development, and growth of society at large. Their ability to act for the betterment of themselves and the world in which they live should be woven into policies and programs at all levels. In the coming decades, many countries are likely to face fiscal and political pressures in relation to public systems of health care, pensions and social protections for a growing older population. By 2005, one in four persons living in Europe and North America could be age 65 or over!

Ironically, COVID-19 is a worldwide wake up call for our global communities and lifestyle. We need only to be move from 3D to 4D in outlook on life and to integrate and balance an aging perspective into the mix of tomorrow's world. Aging is about living mindfully, soulfully and peacefully and about turning the knowledge gleamed from one's life story into wisdom for reconstruction in a new pandemic era.

Almost as if it is a postscript, I have to comment that during the writing this series of 4D Awareness papers, it was discovered that I had cancer and I am now living in my apartment with nursing care as I recover from a major surgery. It is not my first bout with cancer. As we say in my community, "old age is not for sissies."

CONCLUSION: IN THE NEW POST-PANDEMIC ERA

Aging is when we learn to interdependent. But as we get older, this learning intensifies. We have no choice. Our bodies are not the same, more vulnerable and more open to frailties. Our minds are less active. Our social milieu is radically different. And yet our aging is ongoing and with it, our learning. In my community, we call it "our purpose in life."

So once again I have to say that I'm in the right place for me at this time in my life. The admiration where I live is quite open about recognizing its residents as four dimensional with physical, intellectual, emotional and spiritual needs. Given these four dimensions of our learning, it recognizes us as a community and our community as a part of the larger community. Within the constraints of COVID 19, we have been able to stand firm as a community. It happens in so many small ways as well as by collective effort but so far we have been able to live out the days and look toward the future. Moreover, the administration is very aware of the importance of family to us all and again within the constraints of COVID 19, makes visits possible. For that I am very grateful as I am for the visits of my two sons, not just to take me to and from clinics but more important to keep me up to speed on what's happening within the family and community.

Having said all of this, I am even more aware of the change that is happening all around me and of the need to feed my brain more often and differently if I am to be up-to-date in the ongoing development of my humanity. Not so very long ago, I had a telephone conversation with one of my great granddaughters, Jozee. She was only three months old at the time and a very active. My granddaughter showed my picture on the screen of her iPad and I talked into the picture of Jozee on mine. Amazingly, Jozee stopped in front of my image for a good twenty minutes and we made sounds at each other. She is growing up in a very different world than the world I grew up in! I will have to learn to catch up with her and she will have to learn to catch up with me.

Even more recently, another of my great grand daughters, Everlee, "starred" on Facebook. At barely four years old, she announced the imminent arrival of a sibling. So it's an intergenerational thing that we are only beginning to understand and that we will have to work on as we are driven to a new communication in the NEW POST COVID-19 ERA.

Fortunately for me, the administration where I now live is very aware of the importance of family and of community. So even though I am not as technically advanced in terms of my brain power – left versus right – that I can take full advantage of my iPad to talk on the phone with images as well as sounds, I can get help with making the adjustment. But for some reason, I have done it as much as I could have. Hard to get used to.

Regardless, the administration where I live provides iPad sessions upon request, even virtual visits to church along with a continuation of interpersonal programming in the hall at 6 foot distancing. However, I'm old fashioned enough that I prefer to keep in touch with family and friends and with my granddaughters especially by phone. I will have to learn and get control of the new ways of communicating. We all will. Today's technology is only beginning to assist us all in communicating in the NEW POST-PANDEMIC WORLD. But there's more to it than family. There is also our education, our employment, our participation in and contribution to the world that we are building for our humanity.

What is happening to us in the process of our aging under the dictates of a NEW POST-PANDEMIC era will need to be a major part of the rebuilding of services for everyone as we grow older. In fact, it may be a model for the way of all of our institutions and organizations in the NEW POST-PANDEMIC era will need to change. All of us of all ages, colors and creeds will need to be valued equally and respected four dimensionally. Meanwhile, our aging is generating a massive collective intelligence that we have yet to tap into to the fullest extent.

It's the same for all of us – whether we are going to school, to our places of work and to one degree or another of care homes. We are equipped with four levels of intelligence – body, mind, heart and soul – to handle this new learning. And we are generating four level intelligence by learning and sharing our learning. But we need to feel that we are being involved in terms of our ongoing growth and development at all four levels and regardless of our medium of self-expression and learning.

I've tried to express this in a poem.

IN THE NEW POST-PANDEMIC ERA…

LIFE will be…

What we choose to make of it

Versus what it chooses to make of us.

We know this now from our personal and political experience.

MINDFULNESS will be...

All the relevant Knowledge accumulated

And shared thus far as thoughts and ideas.

Science and our Education are telling us so.

SOULFULNESS will be...

All the significant Wisdom revealed

And conveyed thus far as feelings and intuitions.

Spirituality and our Religions guide us still.

PEACEFULNESS will be...

All the Knowledge and Wisdom

Combined as an ever-expanding ONE.

It is a new sense of SELF and OTHERS speaking out.

AGING will be...

Valued as a lifelong process resulting in experiences of
PEACEFULNESS

With paths leading to an ever-increasing awareness of
LOVE and WONDERMENT!

Our choices post-pandemic, MINDFUL and SOULFUL,
will make it so.

It's a matter of our finding a new balance – a new wholeness – that reflects our humanity personally and politically and of our being open to and having access to the new knowledge and wisdom that is carrying us forward one generation to the next as well as one person to another. It is a matter of our being four dimensional in outlook and of our learning from the bottom up as well as from the top down with all eight of our senses fully activated. It is a matter of individual and social conscience and of our working together toward the common good of our humanity as a whole. It is a message of hope.

Made in the USA
Monee, IL
18 June 2021

71665961R00046